# 30- minute therapy

## _for_ ANGER

**everything** you need to know
in the **least** amount of time

Ronald T. Potter-Efron, PhD
Patricia S. Potter-Efron, MS

New Harbinger Publications, Inc.

## Publisher's Note

*This publication is designed to provide accurate and authoritative information in regard to the subject matter covered. It is sold with the understanding that the publisher is not engaged in rendering psychological, financial, legal, or other professional services. If expert assistance or counseling is needed, the services of a competent professional should be sought.*

Distributed in Canada by Raincoast Books

Copyright © 2011 by Ronald T. Potter-Efron and Patricia S. Potter-Efron
        New Harbinger Publications, Inc.
        5674 Shattuck Avenue
        Oakland, CA 94609
        www.newharbinger.com

Cover design by Amy Shoup
Text design by Michele Waters-Kermes
Acquired by Jess O'Brien
Edited by Elisabeth Beller

**FSC**

**Mixed Sources**
Product group from well-managed
forests, controlled sources and
recycled wood or fiber

Cert no. SW-COC-000952
www.fsc.org
© 1996 Forest Stewardship Council

All Rights Reserved. Printed in Canada.

This book in printed with soy ink.

---

Library of Congress Cataloging in Publication Data

Potter-Efron, Ronald T.
  Thirty-minute therapy for anger : everything you need to know in the least amount of time / Ronald T. Potter-Efron and Patricia S. Potter-Efron.
    p. cm.
  ISBN 978-1-60882-029-0 (pbk.) -- ISBN 978-1-60882-030-6 (pdf ebook)
  1. Anger. 2. Control (Psychology) I. Potter-Efron, Patricia S. II. Title.
  BF575.A5P87 2004
  152.4'7--dc22

                               2011002585

13     12     11

10  9  8  7  6  5  4  3  2  1                First printing

# Contents

# Introduction

This book is intended for people who want and need quick guidelines on how to handle specific anger issues. For example, if you have a short fuse, meaning that you get angry really quickly, you'll want to check out chapter 14 on taking a good time-out.

You don't have to define yourself as a person with a bad anger problem to use this book. After all, every human being gets angry from time to time. Most of us get stuck at least once in a while, too, not knowing what to say or do with our anger. The chapters in this book will help you get out of those nettlesome situations.

We've divided the book into three major parts. Part 1 is a group of chapters designed to help you identify your trouble spots. How does your anger cause you and others problems? For instance, do you get too intensely angry when you're upset? Do you have trouble thinking when you're mad? Part 2 will help you set realistic goals to deal with your anger. Part 3 handles the nitty-gritty stuff: specific techniques you can use to manage your anger, including chapters on identifying other emotions you have in addition to anger and putting yourself in someone else's shoes, and even a chapter on self-forgiveness in case you direct a lot of anger at yourself.

Each chapter is divided into three units. The first section is a brief introduction to the topic that usually includes at least one clear way you can deal effectively with your anger problem. Then we'll add more information in the second section, including more helpful ideas for your consideration. Finally, in the third section, which is available online at http://20290.nhpubs.com, we offer extra suggestions, some examples of how people have successfully dealt with their anger problems, and longer exercises that will help you better understand your anger and change your behavior.

We've included many exercises in these chapters. Some of them ask you only to think carefully about a particular situation or concern. At other times, we ask you to write down your ideas in this book or on a notepad. As always, the more you put into this effort, the more you'll get from it.

# Part 1

# Identify Your Trouble Spots

# 1 Excessive Anger and Its Costs

## What You Need to Know

This book is designed to give readers with at least some anger problems quick and effective ways to control their anger. Since you are reading this book, you probably realize your anger is creating problems, sometimes serious ones, in your life—and you're no longer minimizing the problem or in denial.

Since anger almost certainly has been causing problems for you and others, let's begin by taking a good look at how your anger and/or aggression may have messed up your life.

- *Your spouse, partner, or past partners*: arguments, breakups, physical violence

- *Your children or stepchildren*: useless fights, loss of love, loss of connection

- *Your family of origin (parents, siblings)*: endless battles, cutoffs where people won't talk with you, physical fights with brothers and sisters

- *At work or school*: arguments with coworkers or schoolmates, getting fired or suspended, failure to get promoted

- *With the law*: police calls, disorderly conduct charges, no-contact orders

- *Your physical or mental health*: increased anxiety and/or depression, anger-related accidents, high blood pressure

- *Your finances*: fines, replacing broken objects, attorney fees, cost of anger management programs

- *Your values and spirituality*: broken promises not to get angry or lose control, guilt and shame after blowups, anger at God

- *Anything else:*_____

..........................................................................

**exercise.** How has your anger and aggression caused you problems?

..........................................................................

# Taking It Further

Here's a suggestion about how you can use your knowledge of the negative effects of your anger to help you plan your changes.

.................................................................................

**exercise.** Go through the items above to decide which things you most need to work on immediately. Please don't say "all of them" because that's probably too much to take on right now. Instead, be selective. Ask yourself this question: Where is my anger causing the most friction, trouble, loss, and pain—both to myself and to others—right now?

*Example*: For instance, if your relationship with your twelve-year-old step-daughter is a disaster that your anger is only making worse, then make a commitment to quit getting angry at her no matter what she says or does. Or maybe you're close to losing your job because of your cynical attitude. So for now, make a promise to yourself to keep those nasty thoughts and comments to yourself at work. That will buy you some time to change at a deeper level— to eventually quit thinking those mean-spirited thoughts and even start thinking more positive thoughts about your coworkers.

.................................................................................

We want to say one thing to you at the very start of this book: you and you alone are in charge of your anger. That's both good and bad, of course. It's good because you can take full responsibility for making your life better. It's bad because you can't blame others for your problems. That's not to say that everybody you know wears halos on their heads. Nobody's perfect. For instance, maybe your partner has bad days during which he or she becomes easily irritated without reason. The key question is what you will do with that behavior. Will you accept these anger invitations and react with anger, sarcasm, and aggression? Or will you pass on them, letting them go because they're not worth getting all upset over? You and you alone will make the decisions that determine how frequently you become angry and how much damage you do to yourself and others with your anger.

More in **Practices and Examples** at http://20290.nhpubs.com

# 2 The Short-Fuse Problem

## What You Need to Know

The anger problem that most frequently gets people into trouble is having a short fuse. Something disturbing takes place and—BOOM—you go off like a firecracker. In fact, your anger develops so quickly that sometimes the firecracker explodes while it's still in your hand.

This problem is also called having a hair-trigger temper. You have a hair trigger when almost anything can upset you, including many things that most everyone else simply ignores.

What are your most common triggers? Your alarm clock ringing at 6:00 a.m.? Your kids arguing at the breakfast table? Someone cutting you off as you drive to work? A coworker's "stupid" remark? A little glitch on a project that keeps you from doing exactly what you want exactly when you want? A small, maybe unintended, criticism your partner makes during dinner? Not being able to find the television remote control? A nighttime call from a telephone solicitor? Trying to come up with a way to pay your bills when money is tight? Getting grumpy and irritable because you are sleep deprived?

8

How often do you become angry: once an hour, twice a day, every morning, late at night?

..................................................................................

**exercise.** Carry a small notepad and a pencil with you for a week. Start a fresh page every morning. Keep your notepad with you at all times. Then every time you get angry—even just a little angry—make a mark in that notebook. If you have time, you might want to add some information about what was going on that triggered your anger. But that's not absolutely necessary. What's most important is for you to tally up how often you let yourself become angry every day.

..................................................................................

# Taking It Further

Use your notepad to measure success in the future.

..................................................................................

**exercise.** You can use your notepad to measure how frequently you say and do positive things that prevent or cut off your anger. For example, you might make a check mark (or a longer entry) each time you give praise to someone in your family. Take note of every time-out you take that helps prevent a nasty argument. Write down each time you practice breathing more deeply or a relaxation exercise that helps you stay calm. It's also a good idea to write down in your notepad or a journal the thoughts you use to stay calm in anger-provoking situations. These positive choices help you both stay in control of your anger and replace negative, anger-increasing thoughts and behaviors with positive, anger-reducing ones.

We want to issue a warning, though. Don't expect that you'll be able to completely eliminate your hair-trigger temper. Chances are that it comes on too fast and is too strong for you to keep it from ever occurring. Someone says something negative to you (or at least you think it is negative) and BOOM, here comes that old familiar adrenaline rush. Your muscles start to tense up. You feel a sudden impulse to attack. But now comes the critical point in this potential blowup scenario. Just because you've got an adrenaline rush doesn't mean you must act on it. Just let the adrenaline course through your veins. Notice the feeling. Observe it from a little distance almost as if it were happening to someone else. It will probably only take a half minute or so for the adrenaline surge to begin dissipating. Pretty soon it will be gone, just like it was a cloud in the sky. Sure, you'll miss an opportunity to let someone have it for whatever they said or did. But who cares? What's really important is that you gained mastery over the impulse to attack. And that's exactly what anger management is all about.

..................................................................................................

More in **Practices and Examples** at http://20290.nhpubs.com

# 3 The Intensity Problem and Rating Your Anger

## What You Need to Know

Anger is an emotion. It tells you that something is going wrong. It gives you the energy to take action. Anger can help you reach your goals. But it is important to keep your anger in proper perspective. Otherwise you'll find yourself getting really upset over trivial insults. Then you'll overreact.

On a scale from 0 to 10, how strongly would you rate your anger right now, where 0 is "I'm not angry at all," 5 is "I'm fairly mad but still well in control," and 10 is "I'm so furious I'm completely out of control"?

People with anger problems consistently rate their anger as a 7, 8, 9, or 10. It's as if they seldom experience a little anger. Instead, they tend to become highly angry over even apparently little offenses.

So here is another question: On a scale from 0 to 10, how serious is the problem that is triggering your anger?

Do you see where we're going? You have a significant anger problem if you consistently rate your anger high when the problem is small.

## Taking It Further

The *heat index* is another way to rate your anger. When people talk about their anger, they often use a lot of temperature analogies: "I was boiling hot." "I kept my cool." "I was hotter than a pistol." "I stayed cool as a cucumber." "I was steaming mad." "I was hot under the collar." These heat references make a lot of sense. Your body does heat up when you're angry because anger is a response to a perceived threat or danger. Dangerous situations trigger the *fight-or-flight* response, calling on your body to provide energy to make your legs run, your arms strong, and your whole system ready for action. It's natural to feel hot when bothered.

If the numeric scale of 0 to 10 in section A doesn't mean much to you when rating your anger, try this instead: Ask yourself how hot you're getting about the situation. And while you're at it, you might want to ask yourself if you need to cool down a little before you say or do anything.

You may want to design your own personal *anger thermometer* to help you decide just how angry you are in any situation. Put words that you would use to describe how hot you are along a vertical dimension. Your thermometer might look like this:

## Your Anger Thermometer

White-hot

Red-hot

Broiling

Burning

Scorching

Steaming

Toasting

Lukewarm

Cool

More in **Practices and Examples** at http://20290.nhpubs.com

# 4 Thinking or Planning When Angry

## What You Need to Know

The most critical part of the brain for thinking and planning is called the *frontal cortex*, and that's what you need to use in order to think and plan. Unfortunately, when you become very angry you lose the ability to fully utilize that part of your brain. You simply become too excited. Your adrenal gland is shooting out so much adrenaline by then that you've turned from a high-level thinking machine into a defensive, survival-oriented animal. Later you'll remember how much you love and respect the person with whom you're so angry. You'll regret what you've said and done while under the influence of your survival instincts. But right now, with your pulse rate rising, your heart racing, and your voice getting louder, you view that individual as an enemy.

Here's the bottom line: during a conflict you must recognize when you've reached a point where you can no longer think, plan, or problem solve. You can do that by *paying attention to your body*. If you have reached that point, then you need to take a time-out until you have recovered your poise.

..............................................................................

**exercise.** Pay extra attention to your body the next time you get angry. The next section will help you learn what to look for.

..............................................................................

## Taking It Further

Paying attention to your face, body, and thoughts will help you stay in control of your mind.

Different people have different signs—facial and bodily cues that let them know they are starting to become too agitated to think well. How familiar are these characteristics?

☐ My eyes narrow, and I can feel myself beginning to glare at the person I'm mad at.

☐ My jaw gets tight.

☐ My face gets red, or I can feel my face getting hot.

☐ My lips and mouth seem to tighten up.

☐ My voice tone changes. (For most people that means speaking louder but for others it means beginning to speak almost in a whisper.)

☐ I start breathing faster, maybe all the way to hyperventilating.

☐ I can feel my heart pounding.

☐ My whole body starts shaking.

☐ My hands seem to want to turn into fists.

☐ I begin pointing my finger right at the other person or making very emphatic gestures.

☐ My gut begins to hurt.

☐ My muscles get so tight they ache as I try to keep from lashing out.

☐ I start moving toward the other person.

☐ Something else (What?) _____

Pay attention to what happens to your reasoning ability too. Which of these things happens to you?

☐ I have trouble getting my words right. The madder I become, the more difficult it gets to say what I want to say. I might stammer or speak too fast or just quit talking entirely.

☐ I start thinking really mean and nasty thoughts about the other person.

☐ I get to the point where all I want to do is win, no matter what it takes.

☐ I get so mad I don't even hear what the other person is saying, much less actually pay attention to his or her ideas.

☐ I start swearing, a sure sign that my ability to think is rapidly deteriorating.

☐ I pay more attention to how angry I'm getting than to whatever real issues need to be addressed.

☐ I know I'm losing control, but I don't care.

☐ Something else (what?) _____

Pay attention to these physical and mental cues. They tell you that you cannot think clearly in that moment. You would be wise to use the small part of your thinking brain you have left at these times to get away, rather than to stick around to fight.

More in **Practices and Examples** at http://20290.nhpubs.com

# 5 Reacting Too Quickly or Strongly

## What You Need to Know

I wish I could keep my mouth shut for a couple minutes when I get mad. I often regret the first words I speak.

—Sarah

My wife hates it when I swear a blue streak or throw things around. She says I overreact. But I get so angry I have to do something. Besides, isn't it bad for your health to hold your anger in?

—Tony

Sarah's problem is that she hasn't learned to cut off her immediate negative reaction to something that annoys her. She instantaneously goes from feeling attacked or insulted to counterattacking. Sarah seems to lack an inner voice that would tell her to slow down and think about the situation before she does anything.

Tony acts as if he only has an on/off switch in his brain, rather than a more sophisticated regulator. When he gets mad, he gets intensely mad. And then he overreacts. He says and does things way out of proportion to the problem he's facing. Furthermore, he justifies his anger in two ways. First, he convinces himself he simply must lose his cool. Second, he argues he needs to ventilate his anger for health purposes.

..........................................................................................

**exercise.** Are you like Sarah? If so, then remember this one phrase: *always buy time.* This means that when you're angry, you've got to remember to take some time before you act. Repeat this phrase several times a day for at least a week.

If you're like Tony, here's a phrase for you to remember: *stay in control.* You must take full responsibility for your actions. Swearing a blue streak is a choice, not a necessity. Repeat this phrase several times a day for at least a week.

..........................................................................................

## Taking It Further

The two problems described above—getting angry too quickly and reacting too strongly—are often caused by reacting to an irritating situation as if it were a threatening one.

Your brain is basically misinterpreting the problem and making it a much bigger deal than necessary. It needs to be calmed.

There are two pathways in the brain that handle possibly threatening stimuli. The first is the fast path. Here messages are transported from the hypothalamus directly to the amygdalThe result is immediate action. This pathway is very important if and when you are faced with an immediately dangerous situation, for instance, if you are threatened by a bully on the street.

There is an alternative pathway, though, a slower path that takes longer because it goes through the newer parts of the brain, allowing for higher-level processing. The result is a more measured response. While the fast path works best for immediate danger, such as a truck barreling toward you, the slower path works better for non-life-threatening dangers, including the kind of personal annoyances common in day-to-day living.

You may not be able to keep from having a fast-path reaction since it happens so quickly and is mostly out of your conscious control. Nevertheless, your job with regard to anger control is to make every effort to choose to take the slow path. That will allow you to buy time and to think out better responses to the situations that trigger your anger. Taking a time-out (see chapter 14) is the single best way to reduce your risk of an immediate overreaction.

**exercise.** Here's something else we'd like you to try. Every time you start to get mad, say this to yourself: "Hey, my brain is getting this all wrong. I'm not in danger. I don't need to panic. I don't need to overreact. I need to take my time before I say or do anything." The idea is to very intentionally intercept your brain's overreaction. You can essentially redirect your brain to travel on the slow path instead of the fast path. Now, we realize this is not an easy joOnce the messages start moving on the fast path, your body immediately gets ready for a fight. You will have to be firm with your own brain. Treat it like a kid who needs to be guided onto the correct road. Get that kid off the freeway and into a slow lane. Remember that every time you do this, your brain will get better at seeking the slower pathway first. Gradually you'll need to spend less time redirecting it. Eventually your brain will get the idea and automatically steer itself onto the slow path when you begin getting upset.

More in **Practices and Examples** at http://20290.nhpubs.com

# 6 Getting Too Angry to Listen

## What You Need to Know

Anger is a messenger. It tells you that something is wrong in your life. Anger lets you know that you're in danger or that something is blocking your path. It suggests that you consider taking action to fight the threat or to unblock the path. There's one problem, though. Frequently anger tries giving you these messages by shouting at the top of its lungs: *Listen to me! Listen to me! Listen to me!*

Meanwhile, your partner, your friend, your coworker, your child, your sister or brother, a customer—even a complete stranger—is trying to talk with you about whatever it is that has upset you. He or she wants to try to work with you, to reassure you that you're safe or to negotiate with you about how to remove whatever obstacle is blocking the path. Too bad you can't hear that person. It's as if he or she is trying to talk with you while you are wearing a headset with music blasting in your ears.

You've got to take the headset off. That means turning your anger off or at least turning down the volume enough so you can actually listen to what the other person is saying. Here's how:

1. Take a minibreak to gain time. Go to the restroom. Step outside. Get a snack from the kitchen.

2. When you're alone, take a few deep breaths and try to relax.

3. Say out loud or think to yourself, "Thank you, anger—I've got the message. Please don't shout anymore. I need to think."

4. Return to your conversation, this time really attending to what the other person is saying.

## Taking It Further

Sometimes minibreaks aren't enough. You'll simply not be able to calm yourself enough to have a reasonable conversation no matter how badly you'd like to do so. In that case you will need to take a longer time-out. But why is it so hard to cool off once you've become angry?

Your inability to think well or have a productive conversation when you become quite angry is perfectly normal. Strong anger triggers primitive survival instincts. The goal becomes living through the moment, not negotiating a win-win solution. So your body goes into attack-or-flee mode. Your muscles tense. You become supervigilant. And up goes your blood pressure. Once your blood pressure rises too high, you simply will not be able to have a meaningful conversation. You know about "fight or flight," of course. What happens here, though, is more like "fight or think."

*Flooding* is a good name for this problem. It's like your anger is a river in your mind. Every so often, that river rises above its banks and floods towns with names like "Logic," "Compromise," "Caring," and "Calmness."

Some people are slow to flood. If you could picture their anger rivers, you'd see them flowing slowly and quietly almost all the time. Unfortunately, other individuals must deal with relatively wild rivers, the kind with powerful currents and dangerous rapids. Maybe the worst situation is to have an anger river that runs through a slot canyon like they have in the desert. One minute you're peacefully walking through the deep but narrow canyon. The next second you're fighting for your life as a torrent of water surges through the only channel it's got.

How quickly does the anger flood recede? That depends on your brain and body. Some people we've worked with only need a couple minutes even if they've become quite irate. On the other side of the spectrum, we've met people who need twenty-four to forty-eight hours to calm down once they've flooded.

**exercise.** The critical issue here is how long does it take you to stop flooding? Do you know the answer to that question? If not, measure your pulse rate the next time you get mad. If it's over one hundred beats per minute, take a time-out and try to relax. Keep measuring your pulse rate to see how long it takes before it drops back under one hundred. But notice that if you start thinking about what got you so mad, your pulse rate will probably quickly rise again.

More in **Practices and Examples** at http://20290.nhpubs.com

# 7 Becoming Resentful

## What You Need to Know

Anger is supposed to be a brief signal that something is wrong. The message in anger is this: "Hey, something is blocking my path. I need to push it out of the way." The goal is for you to receive the signal, do something productive, and then let go of your anger.

But what if something goes wrong? For instance, you notice your teenager hasn't cleaned up her room for days. You get angry. You confront her and order her to clean her room. Instead of obeying, she merely grunts and walks away. Three days later her room is still a mess. Now you're really mad. You repeat your orders. She ignores you again and again and again.

Slowly your anger builds into resentment. Think of resentment as extended anger. What should be a sprint has turned into a marathon.

Later we'll describe some ways to deal with resentments, especially by using forgiveness. But for now we'll just identify the main characteristics so you can see if you are burdened by resentment. Let's find out how familiar you are with these traits:

- You feel stuck with angry feelings and thoughts about someone and you can't get rid of those feelings and thoughts.

- You think mostly about the bad things this individual has done while ignoring his or her positive qualities.

- Sometimes you believe that you actually hate the person you resent.

- You see the offender as a bad person instead of someone who has done things you don't like.

- The quality of your life suffers because you spend too much time thinking about the person you dislike.

If one or more of these statements applies to you, then your anger has turned into resentment.

## Taking It Further

"Don't let someone have free rent in your brain." That's a saying we first heard at an open AA meeting many years ago. The speaker, Ed, was addressing his alcoholism. He told us that he had relapsed several times over the last decade. Each time Ed went back to drinking, it was over a resentment that kept growing bigger and bigger over time. At first he said his anger was like a little pebble that kept rolling around in his mind. Then it became the size of a rock, a boulder, and finally a mountain. The larger that resentment became, the more time and energy it demanded. Eventually Ed found himself spending hours every day thinking about how various people—his ex-wife, a former employer, his estranged daughter—had so badly mistreated him. He began thinking of these people as totally evil. He said, "I became utterly consumed with my hatreds." He became overwhelmed as anger took over his brain and his body. And then Ed relapsed. He drank in a desperate effort to forget his pain. But even that effort backfired. "I drank to forget. Instead, the more I drank, the angrier I became. So then I'd drink more to try to forget what my drinking mind was remembering." Fortunately, Ed ended his talk by celebrating the five years he'd stayed sober. His formula for success included taking time every morning and every evening to let go of his resentments and to be grateful for the good things in his life.

Ed's story provides two major lessons:

1. *Hanging on to resentments can ruin your life.* That's always obvious in retrospect. After you've let go of a resentment, you can see what a terrible

waste of time and energy it was. Unfortunately, it never seems that way while you're holding on to resentment. Instead, you feel totally justified in your anger. "Just look at what that guy did to me," you think. "How could I not keep thinking about him? How could I not want revenge? Why should I stop hating him?" Your resentment feels like a life raft in a sea of desperation. What you don't realize at the time is that the water isn't really all that deep. If you'd only let go of that raft, you could easily wade back to shore.

2. *It helps to develop a daily ritual when you need to let go of resentments.* That's because resentments are very sneaky and persistent. Few people can just dismiss a resentment the first time they try. Resentments tend to hang around the edges of your soul, waiting for an opportunity to return (just like addictions, by the way, which is why resentments are such a problem for recovering addicts). Ed developed a twice-daily routine that helped him remember each day to put his gratitude ahead of his resentments and his joy for life ahead of his anger at life.

**exercise.** Are you ready to let go of the life raft of resentment so you can freely swim in the sea of life again? What kind of ritual or routine would help you alleviate your resentments? Here's a place for you to design one.

_____

_____

_____

_____

_____

_____

_____

_____

_____

_____

_____

_____

More in **Practices and Examples** at http://20290.nhpubs.com

# 8 Knowing Your Payoffs

## What You Need to Know

It would be easy to quit being so angry if you were punished every time you blew a gasket. But reality is more complicated than that. You may be reluctant to give up your anger because you receive payoffs (rewards) by getting angry. Perhaps you don't get a payoff every time you get angry—just often enough to keep you going. At any rate, it is important that you become fully aware of how your anger benefits you. Only then can you make an informed decision to give up receiving these payoffs so you can live a better life.

........................................................................................

**exercise.** Here are some common payoffs for getting or staying mad:

- ☐ I get what I want when I get angry.

- ☐ I push people away so I can have some space for myself.

- ☐ Getting angry is my way of making others listen to me.

☐ I force people to leave me alone by becoming angry.

☐ I do things my way—my anger warns people not to tell me what to do.

☐ I feel in control when I get angry.

☐ I avoid other feelings, such as anxiety and sadness, by getting angry.

☐ I gain power over others when I get angry.

☐ I like it that people are afraid of me when I get angry.

☐ I don't have to take responsibility for my actions when I get mad.

☐ I hide feelings of shame, guilt, and low self-worth from myself and others with my anger.

☐ I gain status with my anger—people treat me with greater respect.

☐ I like the strong feelings I have when I get angry. I feel alive and energetic.

☐ People pay more attention to me when I become angry.

Please identify which of the payoffs listed above most apply to you and your anger.

..............................................................................................

# Taking It Further

Okay, so now you know your payoffs. But remember that your payoffs must be balanced against the costs of your anger. This might be a good time for you to go back to the exercise in section A of chapter 1 so you can review the immediate and longer-term penalties you've experienced because of your anger. Think again about the people you've driven away and the financial losses, mental anguish, and unnecessary pain that your anger has cost you. It's pretty likely that these penalties far exceed the rewards for your anger. Why else would you be reading this book?

So why, then, have you hung on to your anger so long when it costs you far more than it rewards you? Maybe the fact that the reward comes first and is only followed later by a penalty keeps you angry. Yell first and regret it later. Immediate gratification often wins out over long-term well-being. Just ask the cocaine addict or compulsive spender about that.

Of course there is another possibility. Perhaps your anger has become such a deeply ingrained habit that you just can't let it go. Becoming angry has become an automatic, unthinking way of reacting to the universe. Maybe you react to almost everything with anger even if that response makes no sense. Your anger has become your "default option" in life, the emotion that is always on until you learn how to turn it off. If so, the payoffs we've described above are only part of the picture. Once a habit develops, it can go on for decades even after it quits being rewarding. Now you get angry just because you get angry.

..................................................................................

**exercise.** Try going twenty-four hours without becoming angry even once. Notice your feelings. Watch your reactions to what others say and do. If you really do have a bad habit of anger, you'll probably notice that it's much harder to quit being angry than you realized. You'll start to get angry so quickly and auto-matically that nasty words will come out of your mouth before you can stop them. If you haven't developed the habit of anger, though, it should be fairly easy to go twenty-four hours without getting angry.

..................................................................................

More in **Practices and Examples** at http://20290.nhpubs.com

# Part 2

# Set
# Realistic
# Goals

# 9 Doing No Harm

## What You Need to Know

We can write forever about controlling, containing, or managing anger. We can describe at least one hundred techniques and tactics that could help you accomplish that task. There are cognitive methods to help you think less angry thoughts and plan better actions. We have other tools to help you explore more positive, optimistic ways to view the world. There are spiritual approaches that help you accept your anger but not act upon it. We'll be presenting some of these tactics and techniques throughout the rest of this book.

The problem is that none of these tools will work until you make a strong and definite commitment to the goal of anger control.

We'll discuss this matter further in section But let's move here to the primary issue. Are you ready, right now, to make a powerful commitment to anger management? Please think about this question carefully. If you just think a quick "Sure, why not?" nothing good will happen. Perhaps you need to review the chapter 1, in which you described how your anger has messed up your life, before going on.

When you are completely prepared, consider making this promise:

........................................................................................

**exercise.** I, _____, commit on this date, _____, to control my anger and aggression. That means I will make every reasonable effort not to become excessively angry no matter what others say or do. I will not allow myself to lose control. I will no longer make excuses for my past or present irresponsible behavior. I will practice new thoughts and behaviors that help me control my anger, and I will do so daily.

........................................................................................

## Taking It Further

The goal you've just made is to develop sound and effective anger management skills. More than that, though, the goal is to alter your brain and your mind. That may seem like a daunting task. If so, it could be helpful for you to think of one bad habit that you've quit or at least curtailed. Perhaps it was smoking cigarettes. Maybe it was the habit of procrastinating, putting things off instead of dealing with them as they arose. Possibly it was a mental habit like being too pessimistic. Or maybe you've let go of the habit of low self-esteem, gradually replacing it with having better feelings about yourself.

Now ask yourself how you accomplished this personal transformation. Probably you combined three things:

1. You made a strong commitment to change.

2. You studied the problem until you knew what you needed to think and do in order to change.

3. You carried through by making the changes you needed to make and sticking with them over time. For instance, you may have quit smoking by committing with all your heart to quit; deciding what option, such as using the patch, would work best for you; and staying away from the store at which you always bought your cigarettes.

That's the formula for success with your anger problem: Make the commitment. Develop a plan. Follow through.

........................................................................................

**exercise.** Now it's time to develop your plan. Since we've already covered the first phase—namely, making a commitment—let's go on to the next phase, selecting the changes you most need to make. Please think through your answers in the following areas:

- *Thought life.* I know I need to think differently about things in order to stay calm. Two thoughts that will really help me do this are

_____

_____

- _Emotional life._ I need to be open to other emotions rather than just let myself become angry all the time. The emotions I most need to allow into my life are

_____

_____

- _Behavior._ My anger leads me to verbal or physical aggression. Instead of aggressing when I become upset, I need to

_____

_____

- _Spirit._ I'm tired of feeling angry, depressed, irritable, and mean-spirited. I'd much rather let myself feel

_____

_____

..............................................................................

More in **Practices and Examples** at http://20290.nhpubs.com

# 10 Your Anger Management Goals

## What You Need to Know

Anger is an emotion that usually occurs in an episodic pattern (as does fear, but not sadness, which follows more of a wavelike, waxing and waning pattern). An episode of anger typically consists of a fairly clear beginning ("She implied I was lazy, and right away that ticked me off"), a surge of emotion that reaches a specific intensity level ("I'd give it about a 6 on my heat meter"), and a definite ending ("I stayed mad about an hour, but then I cooled down"). You can use this information to help you change the ways you handle your anger.

First, you could set a goal of getting angry less often. Perhaps right now you become irritated or worse five times a day on average. Imagine how much your life would improve if you could get that number down to twice a day within a month and eventually down to just once a week.

You could also set a goal of becoming less intensely angry. That would take discipline, of course, but wouldn't you feel better if even when you did get mad you could stay calm enough to think and talk reasonably?

The third goal is to shorten the length of your anger episodes. This one is especially important if you sometimes hang on to your anger for long periods.

We have one more anger management goal to ask you to consider—to do less damage when you become angry. Needless to say, this fourth goal is critical if you have developed the habit of breaking objects, smashing your fist into a wall, striking others when you become angry, or the like. But remember that you can also do a lot of damage to others with mean words. Verbal attacks can be just as devastating to the people we love as physical assaults.

....................................................................................

**exercise.** Please take some time to think about these four goals. How important are they to you? Which one is most important right now? Start with that goal and go from there.

....................................................................................

## Taking It Further

Let's briefly mention a few reasons why it's difficult to meet each of these goals.

- *Getting angry less often.* You may have developed such a strong habit of anger that it comes almost automatically.

- *Becoming less intensely angry.* Your body seems only to have an on/off switch for anger, not a better regulator.

- *Shortening the length of an anger episode.* You have such a strong desire to get in the last word or to win an argument that you can't walk away.

- *Do less damage.* You really want to hurt others when you get mad, so it's hard not to say or do mean things.

. . . . . . . . . . . . . . . . . . . . . . . . . . . . . . . . . . . . . . . . . . . . . . . . . . . . . . . . . . . . . . . . . . . . . . .

**exercise.** Imagine this is "gut-check time." That's when you look fearlessly into your soul to see yourself at your nastiest. Now think about what you're like when you become angry. Can you visualize the mean part of you that really wants to attack and harm others? What's it like? How do you look when you're out to get someone? Most importantly, what are you going to do with your "inner nasty" as you try to cut down on your anger and aggressiveness?

. . . . . . . . . . . . . . . . . . . . . . . . . . . . . . . . . . . . . . . . . . . . . . . . . . . . . . . . . . . . . . . . . . . . . . .

More in **Practices and Examples** at http://20290.nhpubs.com

# 11 The Substitution Principle

## What You Need to Know

People with anger problems usually come to our office with one goal in mind. They want to become less angry. Or, more extreme, they want never to get angry again (which, of course, is impossible). We tell them that's not enough. Lessening their anger represents only half a goal. They also need to come up with a set of positive goals that will replace their old negative thoughts, feelings, and actions. They need to replace all that time with more positive thoughts, feelings, and behaviors. If not, they'll just create a vacuum, a low-energy place where they aren't getting angry but also aren't doing anything positive. We call this process of replacing negative energy with positive energy *the substitution principle.*

Think about how much time you spend every day on your anger because of your grumpy moods, nasty thoughts, mean spirit, and useless arguments. Now ask yourself what you could do with the time that gets freed up as you let go of your excessive anger. See if you can imagine one new behavior, one different thought, and one new mood. For example, the new behavior could be playing ball with your kids. The new thought would be "Hey, this is fun," and the new mood could be feeling happy instead of grumpy around your kids.

## Taking It Further

As simple and obvious as it is, we believe that it is absolutely critical for you to honor the substitution principle. Let's put it clearly: you will not be able to maintain your gains unless you make a serious commitment to change what you say, do, think and feel.

Think about this example: A man named Butch decides to quit drinking. Butch really wants to quit. He sure needs to stop drinking before he ruins his life. So one day Butch quits cold turkey. Great. He's done it. But when you ask Butch how his life is different, he says that nothing has really changed. He really hasn't altered his lifestyle at all. In fact, he still heads to his favorite tavern several times a week "because that's where all my friends hang out and where I have a good time." So what do you think are the chances that Butch will stay sober? We'd guess about one in a hundred, at best.

Butch is a little puzzled, though, because he hasn't seen his pal Lenny lately. That's because Lenny discovered the substitution principle. He's spending the time he used to be at the bar camping with his wife and kids, sharing stories at a self-help group, and working out at the gym. It's pretty clear that Lenny's odds to stay sober are much better than Butch's.

If, like Butch, you hang around angry people and live an angry lifestyle, you'll soon be just as angry as you've ever been. But if you play it smarter and change your lifestyle in significant ways, then you'll probably be able to stay calm. In this way, following the substitution principle is relapse prevention.

Notice that letting go of anger takes more than just altering what's going on inside your brain. You'll need to make serious choices about the people with whom you spend your time. You might have to hang out with different people if your current crew of friends and family are mostly angry or mean. Reducing your anger might result in a whole bunch of changes, some predictable and some unforeseen. It's a little like throwing a stone into a pond. You know there will be ripples, but you don't know exactly where they'll go or what effects they'll have.

..................................................................................................

**exercise.** Here's a difficult question: Are there people in your life who keep throwing fuel on the fire of your anger? If so, what is your plan for dealing with them as you become less angry? Will you see them less often? Will you need to keep away from them entirely? If these people are part of your family, what can you do to minimize negative time and maximize positive communication patterns? Try to think about what is between the extremes of doing nothing at all and hoping for the best versus jettisoning your whole life and completely starting over. But be honest with yourself. What do you need to do to follow the substitution principle and avoid relapse?

........................................................................................

More in **Practices and Examples** at http://20290.nhpubs.com

# 12 Accepting Your Anger

## What You Need to Know

Think of the words people use to describe dealing with their anger problems: "eliminate," "contain," "control," "manage." These words imply that anger is mostly dangerous and bad: anger should be eliminated ("I don't ever want to get angry again"), contained ("I try to hold my anger in and not let others see it"), controlled ("I work hard to keep my anger in check"), or managed ("I'm going to classes to learn how to deal with my anger"). The image here is of a lion tamer using a whip to keep a raging beast at a distance. Turn your head away for one moment and you're dead!

But anger isn't our natural enemy. Anger alerts us to threats, gives us energy, and points us toward action. Anger helps us survive in a sometimes dangerous world. Besides, anger is one of six primary emotions hardwired in our brains, along with fear, joy, sadness, surprise, and disgust. You can't totally eliminate it no matter how hard you try.

There is an alternative to the anger-as-enemy approach. You can learn to accept your anger as an essential part of your being. Now anger is more like your friend, maybe a friend who sometimes acts a little stupid, but nonetheless your friend. And, as you would for any good friend, you'll want to listen carefully when anger speaks to you. Accepting your anger means listening well to your friend's complaints. However, listening doesn't mean you have to act upon those complaints.

...................................................................................

**exercise.** What does accepting your anger instead of fighting it mean to you? Can you think of a simple phrase, such as "Don't fight it—just let it be," that would help you accept your anger?

...................................................................................

## Taking It Further

It is very important to understand the difference between *accepting* your anger and *acting* on it. In a book entitled *ACT on Life Not on Anger* (New Harbinger Publications, 2006), Georg Eifert, Matt McKay, and John Forsyth have written about accepting one's anger without acting on it. *Acceptance* means letting go of the desire to eliminate, contain, control, or manage your anger. Instead, you allow yourself to hear your own angry thoughts and to feel your own angry emotions. It's okay to think about them and let them wash over you. By doing so, you are not just accepting your anger; you are accepting the reality that you are a human being who becomes angry from time to time.

Acceptance doesn't mean you like your anger, though; it means you choose to quit fighting that anger. It's part of you, and you can allow yourself to feel your anger without negative judgment.

But look again at the words of that book title: "act on life, not on anger." The authors state that even as you accept your angry thoughts and feelings, you retain your ability to decide how to act. For example, just because you fully experience your anger at your ex-spouse doesn't mean you have to pick up the phone at 3:00 a.m. to harass him or her. Instead, you can opt to do nothing at all until the feeling passes. Or you can call a friend to talk about your pain. Or you can even choose to pray for your ex.

Acceptance of your anger is actually a positive way to handle it. You're less likely to say or do something you'll regret when you fully accept your anger rather than trying to block that feeling. Accepting your anger lessens the likelihood of a "stuff and blow" incident, which can occur when submerged anger finally breaks through to the surface. Such blowups are also less likely to happen when you accept and process your anger rather than constantly dwelling on it and creating a resentment.

What about the "act on life" part? That's the whole point of acceptance. Remember, we're not talking about accepting your anger as if it were outside of you. Anger is part of you. It's a friend who lives inside your brain. It's you—but not all of you. So by fully accepting your anger as a legitimate aspect of your core being, you are more capable of fully experiencing yourself. Learning to accept all your feelings and thoughts helps you embrace life as a whole. Even better, once you stop fighting your own self, you'll have more good energy with which to experience the world outside yourself. You will indeed be acting on life, not anger.

......................................................................

**exercise.** How have you thought of your anger? Is it like a lion fighting the whip of the lion tamer? Is anger your enemy? What would it take for you to accept your anger? How could it become your friend?

......................................................................

More in **Practices and Examples** at http://20290.nhpubs.com

# Part 3

# Use Your Anger Well

# 13 Anger Invitations

## What You Need to Know

An "anger invitation" is our term for anything that happens (inside your mind and body or in the external world) that you could become angry about. Every day brings many invitations for anger: the driver who cuts you off without warning, waking up with a stomachache, someone carelessly leaving their cell phone on and it rings at the wrong time, your partner asking you to buy groceries on the way home, forgetting someone's name, a problem at work with the forklift or copying machine, and so on.

The trick is to be able to say "No thanks" to most of these anger invitations. If you don't learn that trick, you'll be getting angry many times every day. True, you'll always have a reason for your anger. But think of the time, energy, and effort you'll be wasting on all these anger invitations. Unless you've never met an anger invitation you didn't like, you need to become very selective in accepting these invitations.

So how many invitations do you think you've received in the last twenty-four hours? How many have you accepted?

Do you see any differences between the invitations you've accepted and the ones you've declined?

...................................................................................

**exercise.** Here's the big question: How many anger invitations do you think you'll accept in the next twenty-four hours?

...................................................................................

## Taking It Further

Many anger invitations come from the people in your life. Picture them casting out a fishing line with these anger invitations as bait. Imagine them dangling this bait while trolling down the river of your emotions.

You are the fish. Hopefully, you are a fish that doesn't want to snatch the anger bait. You need to be a smart fish. Be very choosy about what you eat. Swim quietly in the weeds where you are hard to locate. Above all, remember this saying: smart fish don't bite.

"Smart fish don't bite" means these things:

- *Learn to react to others less aggressively*: laugh things off, don't let little things bother you.

- *Don't waste your energy trying to make the river flow your way*: just go with the flow.

- *Choose your battles carefully*: remember, the fish loses most of the time.

- *Learn how and when others are trying to hook you*: don't give them the fun of reeling you in.

- *Stay in control of your choices*: get angry when something is worth fighting for, not just because someone threw a line into the water.

........................................................................................

**exercise.** Can you think of three times recently when you got hooked? What happened?

Will you remember that smart fish don't bite the next times these situations arise?

........................................................................................


More in **Practices and Examples** at http://20290.nhpubs.com

# 14  Taking a Good Time-Out

## What You Need to Know

You are getting angry. You don't want to lose control and say or do something stupid. You need to get away. Here's what to do. Follow the four R's so you can take a good time-out. The four Rs of a good time-out are recognize, retreat, relax, and return.

- *Recognize*: You need to know the early signs that you're beginning to lose control so you can take a good time-out. Typically, these signals might include raising your voice, starting to pace, feeling hot as your blood pressure rises, realizing you're not able to listen to what the other person is saying, having aggressive thoughts and difficulty not turning them into actions, making fists, feeling attacked, and so on. The message is "I better get out of here now before I lose control."

- *Retreat*: Get away now. Go somewhere safe and quiet. That will allow you to calm down so you can think better. A word of caution: Don't go someplace where people will urge on your anger. The purpose of a retreat is to calm down, not rev up.

- *Relax*: Let the anger drain out of your mind and body. You might want to exercise to help that happen. Or read a book. Or go fishing. Don't drink or use drugs, though. You'll probably make things worse instead of better that way.

- *Return*: It's not enough simply to calm down. After you've regained your composure, you need to return so you can try to resolve whatever issue triggered your anger. Note: If your fourth "R" is "run away" instead of "return," you aren't taking a good time-out.

## Taking It Further

The time to plan your time-out is before you need to take one. Once you get angry, you may not be able to think clearly enough to do it right.

........................................................................

**exercise.** Use the four Rs to develop your time-out plan:

- *Recognize*: Write down five signs that you are losing control of your anger. If you can't think of five, ask your partner, family, and friends for help.

- *Retreat*: Assume you're really angry and will need at least thirty minutes to calm down. Where can you go? How will you get there? What's your backup plan in case you can't go to this first place?

- *Relax*: How will you go about letting the anger drain away? Will you go for a walk, do breathing exercises, distract yourself with work or activities, or talk with someone who won't throw fuel on your fire?

- *Return*: You'll need to be willing to talk about what happened without blowing up again. How will you know when you can do that?

Here is a way to think about time-outs that will help you if you like sports. Think of a time-out as if it were a safety playing defense in football. In football not all defenders are placed at the line of scrimmage right next to the offense. Some of them are held back a little ways (the linebackers) and some of them are way back (the safeties).

Imagine your anger as if it were the offensive team's star running back. He gets the ball and blasts through the first line of defenders. He dodges the linebackers. Now all that anger has to do is get past the safety to score. Scoring means he'll get you to have a complete meltdown.

The safety is your time-out. He needs to tackle your anger and hold on. Then it will be your turn with the ball, meaning that you'll be able to return to the relationship game in a calm manner.

Teams need safeties, but you don't want to depend upon them for every play. In the same way, you shouldn't overuse your time-outs. Make sure to call for a time-out only when you actually need to take one. If you overuse time-outs, you'll lose credibility.

More in **Practices and Examples** at http://20290.nhpubs.com

# 15 Breathing and Relaxing in Stressful Situations

## What You Need to Know

One of the best ways to lessen anger is by learning how to breathe and relax in stressful situations. You will need to practice this technique regularly for it to be useful, though. Fortunately, it feels really good to be able to let go of your anger just by altering your breath.

......................................................................

**exercise.** Practice your deep breathing:

1. Find a comfortable, quiet place to sit or lie down.

2. Close your eyes.

3. Give yourself permission to relax and let go of any outside stressors.

4. Slowly inhale through your nose, feeling the good air traveling all the way in. Allow the air to push down your diaphragm.

5. Pause for a count of four, and then exhale slowly through your mouth.

6.  Say "one" to yourself.

7.  Repeat steps 4 and 5. This time say "two" to yourself.

8.  Repeat steps 4 and 5 until you have reached the number ten.

You might prefer starting with ten and working your way down to one.

You might want to say "relax" to yourself during the pause between inhaling and exhaling.

You can eventually shorten the number of breaths you take to three or four so you can use this technique more quickly when needed in real-life situations.

..................................................................................

# Taking It Further

Now practice relaxation. During full body relaxation you quiet you muscles and nervous system. Even better, you quiet your mind. Here's how.

..................................................................................

**exercise.** Breathing well is the first way to stay calm and/or to quiet yourself when you've begun to get angry. But you can do even more when you combine your breathing exercise with full body relaxation.

1.  Start relaxing either from the tip of your toes upward or from the top of your head downward. Use your muscle groups for focus: feet and toes, calves and lower legs, thighs and upper legs, hips and pelvis, stomach muscles, chest area, back, shoulders and neck, jaw, face (especially eyes and temples), forehead and top and back of head.

2.  Remember to keep breathing deeply and slowly as you relax. Take as long as you like, but at least fifteen to twenty minutes so you can really feel your body relaxing.

3.  You might want to add a few calming thoughts to this exercise such as "This feels good," "I have all the time in the world," or "I feel safe."

4.  If your brain insists on thinking worrisome thoughts like "I don't have time to do this" or "What should I make for dinner tonight?" or "This isn't working" or "I'm too busy to relax" or "I'm still mad at so-and-so," just imagine these thoughts being tied to a balloon and drifting away. The idea is not to try to stop having these thoughts but to let them depart because they aren't getting much attention.

5.  You might want to add some visual, auditory, or tactile images to your relaxation exercise. For example, almost everybody has a favorite memory of a time when they felt completely at peace with the world. These memories come with wonderful visual images, sounds, or sensations. For instance,

you might recall a time when you were sitting on an ocean beach, feeling the sun warming you, listening to the waves and watching pelicans flying silently over the waves. Or perhaps you're thinking of a time when you were rocking in your favorite chair, eyes shut, glad to be alive, and happy with the universe. You can increase the power of your relaxation exercise by incorporating images like these.

.......................................................................................

More in **Practices and Examples** at http://20290.nhpubs.com

# 16 Avoiding Anger as a Permanent Condition

## What You Need to Know

Anger, especially when it gets combined with anxiety, can take over your brain. You begin fretting about something that's bugging you, and, like the vine in Jack and the Beanstalk, it grows right before your eyes. Your anger juts skyward at the speed of thought. It grows wider and wider, too, so pretty soon you can't see or think about anything else. Your anger fills up your universe. It becomes the only thing in your life that matters. Like a bulldog, your anger won't let go. Worse yet, the longer it goes on, the stronger it becomes, so your fretting turns into fuming. And that means you can no longer think of any good solutions to the problem—your emotions have trumped your thinking ability. You have become obsessed.

..................................................................................................

**exercise.** In chapter 3, we discussed how to keep your anger in perspective by rating your anger on a scale from 0 to 10 or using an anger thermometer to gauge of the seriousness of the problem. But here's another approach.

Think of at least three brief thoughts that can help you remember not to obsess. Here are a few:

> "This is a real problem, but it isn't about life and death."

> "It's time to think about something good in my life."

> "Let go and let God."

> "I won't let my anger run my life."

> "I won't let my anger ruin my life."

Write these thoughts down. Keep them in your wallet, pocket, or purse. Read them every morning or whenever you start getting angry.

# Taking It Further

Who is driving the bus of your life?

Obsessive anger leads to chronic anger. Once you start obsessing about how people have harmed you or whatever else triggers your anger, it gradually takes over your life. Anger can dominate your thinking. It becomes so strong and tenacious that it's almost like you become your anger. "I am my anger and my anger is me" becomes the theme song of your life.

Think of your life as a long bus trip. You are the driver of the bus, but you're not all alone. You have some very interesting passengers. They are your emotions: anger, joy, sadness, fear, shame, guilt, loneliness, and so on. Once in a while you let each of them sit next to you as you drive, but you are in charge of the bus.

Then something strange happens. Your anger stands up, strides to the front, grabs you by the neck, and throws you out of the driver's seat. "I'm hijacking this bus," anger announces, and then orders you to take a seat in the back.

What next? You're in for a wild ride. Your anger will go fast and furious while aiming for every pothole in the road. "Whee, what fun!" anger shouts. But somehow you're not really enjoying the ride all that much.

Then anger stops the bus and glares at your other emotions. Anger tells them to get off the bus: "We don't need any other feelings—I can handle whatever comes up." And so anger does. When your friend waves hello, your anger practically runs her down because you remember a time when she said something mean to you. When you see a family member sitting by the road waiting for a ride, your anger drives on by without a second glance. "Let her walk, she means nothing to me," says your anger, because anger is incapable of empathy.

........................................................................................

**exercise.** What does the bus of your life look like? Has anger taken it over? If so, you need to act assertively. Stand up, walk to the front, and firmly order your anger to get out of that driver's seat. Tell anger that you're back in control of your life. Don't kick anger off the bus, though. Remember that anger can be useful to you, as long as it only comes up to the front when needed and you remain in that driver's seat even when anger is present.

You have one more job, of course. You need to round up the rest of your emotions and invite them back on the bus. Ask yourself which emotion you need to have get back on the bus first. And why is that?

........................................................................................

More in **Practices and Examples** at http://20290.nhpubs.com

# 17 Putting Yourself in Someone Else's Shoes

## What You Need to Know

*Empathy* is the ability to get outside your own worldview temporarily so you can see, feel, and understand the world from somebody else's perspective. The evidence is clear and convincing: people who can put themselves in another's shoes for a while are much less likely to get into useless arguments and unnecessary conflicts. You can definitely improve your empathy skills by taking the time on a regular basis to practice placing yourself in the mind and emotions of another.

You'll need to improve two skills to get good at empathy: being curious and being nonjudgmental.

...................................................................................

**exercise.** The next time you get stuck in an argument, try to put yourself in the other person's shoes. It will help to ask yourself these questions:

- Am I being judgmental? If so, could I place my judgments on hold for a while?

- What is most important to the other person? What are his or her main values?

- What is he or she feeling right now?

- Have I ever been in a similar situation that would help me understand his or her viewpoint?

........................................................................................

# Taking It Further

Becoming more empathic isn't just about learning how to ask questions ("What are you feeling?") or how to be less judgmental. It's deeper than that. The real goal is to better comprehend the other person's life story.

A life story is the way an individual organizes the key events in their lives into a single, meaningful narrative. Let's say that Helen and Michelle each had the same three critical events occur in their teens. Both of them lost their mothers to cancer, suffered through their father's subsequent depression and bout of alcoholism, and had to work long hours during high school to buy their own clothes because of their father's disability. Although the histories of these two women are similar, you can discover, by asking them to tell you their life stories, how different they are.

Helen has put those events together by constructing a narrative in which her main goal in life is to care for others.

She never went to college. Instead, she married early and is lovingly raising a family. Taking care of her father triggered maternal feelings that have become the center of her life. If you were to ask Helen what she had learned from her upbringing, she would say that family means everything.

Meanwhile, Michelle created an entirely different meaning from the same events. She considers herself a survivor, someone who is tough, strong, and capable of anything. She's become a career woman who specializes in troubleshooting difficult situations. The meaning to her of her childhood is that you can't count on anybody to be there for you. Consequently, she relies exclusively upon herself. Yes, sometimes she feels lonely, but she's unwilling to risk the pain of losing yet another person she loves.

You'll never hear Helen or Michelle's life story unless you ask her to tell it. That's what empathy is about. When you listen to another's life story with curiosity and without judgment, you are mastering the art of empathy.

........................................................................................

**exercise.** Ask a couple of people to tell you their life stories. If they ask you what you mean, tell them you'd like to hear about a few of the important events in their lives that helped make them the people they are today.

........................................................................................

More in **Practices and Examples** at http://20290.nhpubs.com

# 18 Replacing Negative Thoughts with Positive Ones

## What You Need to Know

Angry people are awfully good at thinking negatively about what others say and do. Here's a way to change that pattern of thinking.

Classic cognitive behavioral therapy begins with these thoughts:

1. Events just happen.

2. We humans create meaning for events.

3. That meaning can be negative, positive, or neutral.

4. Angry people create far more negative meaning than needed.

5. This leads them to unnecessary hostile actions or remarks.

6. But people can learn to change their thinking from negative to positive and in this way avoid habitual anger.

Here's the technique you need to make this change:

1. An event occurs.

2. You notice you are automatically making a negative interpretation of it.

3. This would normally lead to you saying or doing something hostile.

4. Instead, you choose to make a more positive (or at least neutral) interpretation of the event.

5. And this leads you to respond with less anger or hostility.

*Example*:

1. A guy is driving at 55 mph in a 55 mph lane.

2. You think, "He's slowing me down. What a moron!"

3. You would normally blow the horn, give him the finger, and stay mad for an hour or more.

4. You catch that negative thought and replace it with, "I'm not in a hurry, so why get upset?"

5. You calm down and wait patiently for a good opportunity to pass him.

..................................................................................................

**exercise.** Think of one recent situation in which you became angry. See if you can use this method to change how you would react to the same situation the next time it occurs.

..................................................................................................

# Taking It Further

You may need to change how you look at the world in order to really change the way you think. You may be a person who habitually thinks about life in an unrealistically negative fashion.

Many angry individuals operate in a very negative world. They basically misinterpret the motives of others on a regular basis. Here's how they do this.

First, they don't take in positive comments from others. For example, you bake a chocolate cake and your partner says, "That's nice that you baked a cake." You don't take that compliment very well. In fact, you might interpret your partner's statement as a cynical remark. Or you might be confused, wondering why your partner would say something nice and expecting it to be followed by a criticism.

Second, they hear neutral statements as if they were really criticisms. Suppose your partner had said, "Oh, you baked a cake." You might interpret that negatively and respond, "Well, of course I baked a cake. It's right there on the table. Are you saying I did something wrong? Are you making fun of me?" Now this is a big problem, because the great majority of stuff we say to each other is neutral, neither positive nor negative. People who hear neutral statements as negative ones get upset a lot for no good reason.

Third, they hear low-level negative remarks as if they were total attacks. That's how "I like your cake, but next time please add some frosting" becomes interpreted as "You idiot! What's wrong with you? Any fool would know that cakes need frosting. You are the world's worst baker. And furthermore, you are a hopeless loser."

This whole pattern of misinterpretations is named the *hostile attributional shift.* You'll need to work hard to change this pattern if you realize you have fallen into it.

But there is good news. You can learn to recognize your habitual negative thinking. And then you can challenge your hostile assumptions and replace them by using the method in section A.

.................................................................

**exercise.** Here's today's challenge. See how many negative thoughts you have over the next twenty-four hours and try substituting more positive ones whenever you can.

.................................................................

More in **Practices and Examples** at http://20290.nhpubs.com

# 19 Identifying Your Other Emotions

## What You Need to Know

Life would be simple indeed if we only had to encounter one emotion at a time. It's lots easier to deal with "Right now I feel angry" than with "Right now I feel angry and sad and a little lonely too." But in reality, people usually feel a blend of emotions rather than just one. For instance, as my father lies dying, I might feel terribly sad to see him go but also relieved that his suffering is almost over. I might be afraid of the future ("Now who is going to take care of Mother?"). I might even start laughing as I remember some of the playful things my father and I did while I was a child. Life is full of complex, intermingled feelings.

Think of a recent situation in which you became angry. Now ask yourself what other emotions might have been present that you either didn't notice at all or basically ignored. Perhaps, for example, you had an argument with your partner about his or her drinking. You became irate and let your partner know it. But now, after that scene has passed, you realize that you never told your partner that you were also scared, sad, and lonely. Think of how your conversation could have gone very differently if you had brought these other emotions to the table.

# Taking It Further

Here is an analogy that will help you remember to scan for all your emotions when you get angry. Think about all those old-time Westerns that featured a hero such as the Lone Ranger or Hopalong Cassidy. Sure, those heroes did spectacular things. But didn't they usually have buddies or sidekicks who rode with them, helped gather information, added a needed touch of humor to the hero's often grim challenges, and sometimes even saved the hero's life? Where would the Lone Ranger be without Tonto, or Hopalong without Gabby Hayes? And don't forget the posses, those gangs of good guys chasing after villains. Where would your anger be without all your other feelings? While anger may stand in front, feelings of sadness, fear, excitement, hopelessness, love, hurt, loneliness, and disappointment may be there too, right behind.

We do want to issue a warning: do not buy into the idea that anger is only a cover emotion. When people say that, they mean that anger isn't a real emotion or isn't important except as a way to hide your real emotions. For instance, someone might say that a teen who looks very angry because she can't go out one evening is actually not angry but is hurt or sad or afraid. It may be true that the teen is also hurt or sad or afraid. But that kid is truly angry as well. It's much better to ask that teen, and yourself, what emotions are present in addition to anger rather than to throw away the anger as if it were just the shrink-wrap you peeled off a container to get to the stuff inside.

Don't rely upon anger to do all your emotional work. Allow a few of the other emotions there to be present when you need to tell others what is troubling you. You'll almost certainly find that people will listen and respond better to you when you do so.

Does the analogy with old-time Westerns work for you? Could you think of better ones that will help you remember always to scan for your other emotions when you feel angry?

More in **Practices and Examples** at http://20290.nhpubs.com

# 20 Looking for the Good Instead of the Bad

## What You Need to Know

Here's Harry's reaction when his girlfriend Clarice advises him to look for the good in people:

> Look for the good instead of the bad. Sure, sure. What a trite saying. Look for the good and you will find it. That's what people are always telling me. Frankly, I think it's a bunch of malarkey. Face it. People are mean, nasty, dangerous, untrustworthy, scheming, stupid, ugly, and self-centered. Yes, I could look for the good in them, but why bother? People who say nice things are just trying to use me. People who do me favors are setting me up. There's way more bad than good in this world, and you and I both need to remember that fact in order to survive.

How accurate is this view of the world? Are people all that bad? There is certainly some truth in his argument. But Harry's vision of the world is clouded by his assumption that people are way more bad than good. Since he presumes the worst, he will inevitably find the worst. Harry's self-fulfilling prophecy dooms him to a life of negativity, suspiciousness, and defensiveness.

So what about you? How much do you agree with Harry? How often do you find yourself caught in the circle of finding only the bad things in others because you are only looking for bad things? Do you remember the last time this sequence occurred in your life? If you could replay that sequence and look for the good in people instead of the bad, how might things have turned out differently?

## Taking It Further

*Positive psychology* is a recent development in the field of psychology. Here the focus is on what's good about people rather than on their problems and deficits. For example, positive psychologists study such traits as honesty, courage, leadership, creativity, and reliability. What's amazing is that it's taken so long for this positive approach to emerge. It seems that the whole field is biased toward the negative. Maybe all psychologists need to take a class in anger management so they can learn to look on the bright side of life.

So what kind of psychologist would you rather see? Would it be someone who starts looking for what is wrong with you from the moment you enter the office? Or would it be someone who studied you to locate your strengths and positive qualities. For that matter, which kind of psychologist would you be if you had the opportunity?

........................................................................

**exercise.** Today, go to a place where there are a lot of people, such as a park, restaurant, or family gathering. For fifteen minutes, look for everything you can that's wrong with these people: their clothes, faces, gestures, words, mannerisms, ways of walking—anything and everything. Make things up if you have to. Then check in with yourself. How does seeking the negative feel?

Now take a few deep breaths and switch gears. Start looking for good stuff. Keep that up for fifteen minutes and then think about it.

It would be even better if can you do this exercise with a buddy who would write down your comments as you speak them out loud and then help you process the exercise after you complete it.

Tomorrow, change the exercise this way: only spend ten minutes on the negative start and then twenty minutes on the positive. The third day do five negative minutes and twenty-five positive ones. Then try thirty minutes of straight positive searching.

........................................................................

More in **Practices and Examples** at http://20290.nhpubs.com

# 21 Defusing a Potential Conflict

## What You Need to Know

Here are thirty-nine ways to defuse a potential conflict. Use them when you sense an argument coming on that you want to avoid:

1. Just walk away.

2. Apologize.

3. Take three deep breaths.

4. Look for a compromise.

5. Tell yourself this is no big deal (not a crisis).

6. Sit down.

7. Talk softly and slowly.

8. Give a compliment.

9. Acknowledge the other's view ("You have a point there…).

10. Make a joke to lighten the mood.

11. Remind yourself that smart fish don't bite. You can say no to anger invitations.

12. Step back a little.

13. Stop drinking.

14. Give gentle touch.

15. Put yourself in the other person's shoes.

16. Take a time-out (remember the four Rs: recognize, retreat, relax, return).

17. Commit to being loving instead of warring. Don't treat the people you care about like enemies.

18. Think of something you like about the other person.

19. Make a small concession ("All right, I'll do that the way you want me to").

20. Argue the other person's side (to gain understanding).

21. Tell yourself to cool down—and then cool down.

22. Let the other person have the last word.

23. Focus on solutions, not victories or defeats.

24. Do something different, to break the escalation pattern.

25. Remind yourself to stay in control.

26. Stay in the present.

27. Keep your mouth shut instead of hurling insults.

28. Think in both/and terms instead of either/or.

29. Ask yourself what a calm friend would do in this situation.

30. Don't take things too personally.

31. Take the other person's concerns seriously.

32. Think, "I'm okay; you're okay."

33. Act as if you were calm—and pretty soon you will be.

34. Treat your hot thoughts like clouds in the sky that will soon disappear.

35. Remember what could happen if you say or do something stupid.

36. Make yourself really listen.

37. Do something nice (like bringing the other person a cup of coffee).

38. Respond to an attack with caring and compassion.

39. If this is your partner or child, remember that you love him or her.

## Taking It Further

Okay, you start getting angry. But you can stop yourself if you just keep your head.

We've supplied thirty-nine ways for you to keep a disagreement from escalating into a fight. It's up to you to utilize them. To do so you'll need to recognize the signs that you are starting to become angry as well as the indicators that you and the person with whom you are talking are getting into dangerous territory. When either of you are starting to get loud, repeating your statements, becoming physically agitated, talking without listening, blaming or shaming the other person, and so on, it's time to get out the list above and select one to use.

........................................................................

**exercise.** We'd like you to go through the list above. Select five or six items that you believe would be most helpful when you have a disagreement with your partner, friend, parent, coworker, or whomever you are thinking about right now. Don't just select the techniques you are most familiar with, though. Choose one or two techniques that would be new for you. For instance, you might pick "Respond to an attack with caring and compassion" if normally you are a very competitive individual who would be inclined to respond to an attack with a counterattack. Or perhaps you could try "Think of something you like about the other person" if you would usually do just the opposite during a dispute.

Write down these five or six techniques on a small card that you can carry with you. Look at the card at least twice a day. Then, when it's crunch time, at the beginning of a disagreement, you'll be able to review the list in your mind and choose one to use.

..............................................................................................

Are you familiar with the saying "If you only have a hammer in your tool kit, then every problem becomes a nail"? That saying is relevant here because there are no miracle techniques that work every time. That's why you need to have many tools in your anger management tool kit. So don't rely on any single one of these tools for every situation in which you find yourself. Use the five or six you've selected to find out which ones work best with different people and for you. And don't hesitate to return to the list and select other techniques to try as you master or reject the first five or six.

**exercise.** Here's the ultimate challenge for you. Look through the list one more time. Locate the three techniques that you think would be hardest for you to pull off. Ask yourself why that would be. For example, perhaps "Stay in the present" would be very difficult for you because you're so good at bringing up the past during a disagreement. Put one of these three on your short list and commit to trying it out soon. You might discover you are more flexible than you thought, as well as better at handling your anger.

More in **Practices and Examples** at http://20290.nhpubs.com

# 22 Using "I" Statements

## What You Need to Know

The purpose of an "I" statement is to clearly tell someone exactly what bothers you, how you feel, and what you want changed. There are three parts:

1. *State what the other person has said or done that bothers you:* "Yesterday you promised to talk with me this morning about our financial situation, but you slept in instead."

2. *Tell the other person what you are feeling:* "I'm feeling angry and hurt. Plus I'm worried because we really do need to figure out how to pay the bills."

3. *Now say exactly what you want:* "And I want you to sit down with me this afternoon so we can decide what to do today."

**exercise.** Think of a situation going on in your life right now in which you could use an "I" statement. Now decide what words you could use for each of the three parts.

# Taking It Further

"I" statements look easy. But be wary of making these mistakes:

- *Don't be vague about what's bothering you, how you feel, or what you want.* It's useless to say something like this: "Larry, you're kinda mean to me, and I sorta feel bad, and I want you to be nicer." You need to give Larry much more specific information about what he says that sounds mean, what you mean when you say you feel bad, and how he could say nicer things to you.

- *Don't say, "You make me feel …"* Your feelings are your responsibility, not the other person's.

- *Don't call names or be insulting.* Larry probably won't respond to your "I" statement very positively if you begin with "Larry, you lazy worm,…"

- *Don't expect miracles.* Just because you're using clear language doesn't guarantee you'll get what you want.

- *Don't use "I" statements only to complain.* People often think of using "I" statements only when something bothers them. But why should we limit the use of this powerful technique to negative situations? Why not utilize them to reward somebody for positive behavior?

- "Sally, yesterday you offered to take the kids to the zoo even though you had worked hard all day."

- "I feel great when you take time with them. It warms my heart when I see them playing with you."

- "Next time you go to the zoo, I'd like to go with you and the kids just to watch you having a good time together."

- Everybody needs praise. "I" statements allow you to fine-tune your praise so the recipient learns exactly what he or she is doing that you like.

- *Don't follow a positive "I" statement with the word "but."* For instance in the situation above, don't add "…but you don't do enough with the kids most of the time." Now you've turned praise into criticism. Criticism just makes the recipient defensive, especially when it comes in a surprise attack.

- *Don't turn "I" statements into personality attacks.* Personality attacks are negative statements about some general characteristic of another individual. They often take the form of a "you" statement instead of an "I" statement: "You are so lazy." "You're a jerk." "You're stupid." Using them might make you feel better for a minute because hurting someone you're mad at can be satisfying. However, these kind of assaults almost certainly will increase ill will. Besides, they are virtually useless in terms of actually getting someone to alter their behavior. Who would voluntarily change because someone is calling them names? Most people will do more of the same, not less, when insulted.

There's another problem with personality attacks. They shift responsibility for your feelings, thoughts, and actions off you and onto the other person. You think, "If only that person would quit being a jerk, then everything would be fine." But what about you? Are you doing things that make the situation worse? Blaming the other party almost certainly won't help make things better nearly as much as you deciding how you can change the way you respond to the other person.

More in **Practices and Examples** at http://20290.nhpubs.com

# 23 Fair-Fighting Guidelines

## What You Need to Know

All people disagree from time to time. That means a certain amount of conflict is almost inevitable. However, you can greatly affect the likelihood that your conflict will eventually have a positive result if you fight fair. A positive result occurs when the issue is resolved, at least for a while, and neither person's feelings are hurt during the discussion.

We'll begin this chapter with a list of the things you should avoid doing during the disagreement. Take a good look at them and decide which of these negative behaviors you need to stop.

### Fair Fighting: Don'ts

* *Don't make fun of others.* "You're so cute when you get mad."

* *Don't run away from the issue.* "I don't want to talk about it."

* *Don't overgeneralize.* "You are always late."

- *Don't be dismissive.* "Whatever!"

- *Don't insist on getting in the last word.* "I've got to say one more thing…"

- *Don't get stuck in the past.* "I'll never forget what you said last year."

- *Don't hit, push, shove, or threaten.* "If you say that again, I'm gonna…"

- *Don't stand up and yell or swear.* "@#^$%#!!"

- *Don't interrupt.* "I'm going to jump in here."

- *Don't make faces.* "What do you mean I made a face? I can't help it if I rolled my eyes."

- *Don't attack the other's personality.* "You're a loser and a horrible person."

## Taking It Further

You need to do more than just refrain from the negative communication patterns above, though. You'll need to develop some positive communication skills during disagreements if you really want to solve your conflicts rather than have them go on and on. Try to do the following things during conflict.

...........................................................................

## Fair Fighting: Do's

- *Stick to one issue at a time.* "Let's just talk about money right now. Then we can get to the kids."

- *Sit down and talk quietly.* "I better sit down and calm myself before we start talking."

- *State your feelings clearly.* "When you yell at me, I feel hurt."

- *Listen.* "I think I get your meaning. Let me repeat it to be sure."

- *Be clear and specific.* "I can tell you exactly what I want you to do tomorrow at the bank."

- *Stay flexible.* "I guess I'm being a little rigid now. Let me think about your idea."

- *Be willing to negotiate and compromise.* "Okay, here's a possible compromise."

- *Breathe calmly and stay relaxed.* "I better take a few deep breaths about now to stay relaxed."

- *Take responsibility for everything you say and do.* "I said it, so I can't just take it back like the words never came out."

- *Focus on solutions, not victories and defeats.* "Let's find a way for both of us to be happy about this issue."

- *Take time-outs as needed.* "I'm starting to get too emotional. I need a time-out."

More in **Practices and Examples** at http://20290.nhpubs.com

# 24    Using Your Anger to Fight for a Cause

## What You Need to Know

You can use anger to fight for what is most important to you. "Advocacy" is the name for this effort. Think about Martin Luther King Jr. and the civil rights battle or Gandhi in IndiFor that matter, consider any man or woman who has risked losing a job to blow the whistle on illegal or unethical behavior by an employer.

Advocacy takes courage. You also need to use your intelligence, prudence, and patience to be effective as an advocate. Anger alone isn't enough. You must match your emotions with discipline.

......................................................................................................

**exercise.** Here is a quick thought exercise that will help you identify what situations could lead you to become an advocate for some cause or belief:

- For what cause would you fight?

- For what cause would you risk losing your job?

- For what cause would you risk going to prison?

- For what cause would you risk losing your marriage or significant relationship?

- For what cause would you risk losing your life?

- How about in the past? Have you ever risked losing a lot to stand up for what you believed? If so, how do you feel about what you did back then? Would you do the same things now?

..................................................................................

# Taking It Further

Here are some keys to effective advocacy:

- *Use your emotions but don't get caught up in them.* There is no such thing as dispassionate advocacy. If you really believe in a cause, you'll feel it in your gut. But be careful. It's easy to get carried away because of your strong emotions. You could do a lot of damage to yourself and your cause if you get too emotional. Stay disciplined. Guide your emotions instead of letting them guide you.

- *Know what you're fighting for.* Make a positive value statement. It's not enough to be against something. You have to be for something to fight effectively. That's why people are "pro-life" and "pro-choice" in the abortion debate.

- *Make a long-term commitment.* If something's worth fighting for, then it's worth a long-term commitment. So think carefully about your choices. Prepare yourself to take part in a marathon, not a sprint.

- *Work with others.* Advocacy is a difficult and sometimes lonely undertaking. Many people won't understand why you feel so passionately about your cause. It's important to find others who share your beliefs, both for emotional support and for practical considerations. The Internet can be helpful here (just be careful to avoid "nutcases").

- *Plan carefully.* Learn all you can before you act.

- *Knowledge is critical.* Imagine you're entering into a debate with a proponent of the opposite viewpoint. Sure, you have to present yourself well. But it's not all about appearances. The person who has done the most homework, the one best prepared for the debate, will usually emerge as the winner.

- *Ask yourself what price you're willing to pay.* Know your bottom line.

It's critical for you to decide how far you'll go in the name of the cause you're advocating. Are you willing to go to jail, to lose your job, to be scorned, or to be attacked verbally or physically? There's no correct answer to these questions. But you need to think carefully about them both before you become involved.

More in **Practices and Examples** at http://20290.nhpubs.com

# 25 Deep Resentments and the Need to Forgive

## What You Need to Know

Deep resentments develop when someone says or does something that seriously hurts you and the injury gets stuck in your head. You can't let go of it. Gradually it takes up more and more space in your mind until it completely colors the way you think about and act toward the offender. Ultimately, strong resentment can turn into hatred, which means you despise the person who harmed you. You've turned that individual into someone bad, evil, awful, beyond redemption.

Forgiveness is the key to ending a deep resentment. Forgiveness is an act of generosity on your part. It can never be earned by the offender. When you choose to forgive, you take the offender back into your heart by focusing on the other's humanity instead of how he or she harmed you. Forgiveness is never fast or easy. But here are a few things you can do to help you get a good start on the process:

- Make a clear and conscious decision to forgive.

- Quit blaming the offender for your unhappiness.

- Stop thinking about or doing anything in the name of revenge.

- Let go of any demands you've made for an apology or other form of repayment by the offender. Basically, rip up his or her debts.

- Think about some of the good things the offender has done without immediately going on to the bad things.

- Imagine what it would be like to allow the offender back into your heart.

## Taking It Further

What if you alternate between forgiveness and hate? What if you're not ready to forgive? What if you can't forgive at all? Does forgiving mean getting back together?

Forgiveness is a long and slow process. That's because the offender has done things to you that have deeply wounded you. It's actually quite common to engage in several rounds of forgiveness. First you make a conscious effort to forgive and feel like you've succeeded, and then once again you experience a surge of the old anger and hostility toward the offender. That's normal, so don't be discouraged. Forgiveness isn't an all-or-none event. It's more like a series of efforts in which you gradually achieve lasting peace of mind.

You may not be ready to forgive yet. That's okay. Do not let anybody tell you that you must forgive the offender right now. Forgiveness often backfires when it is shoved at you. You'll know when you're ready. You'll hear a message coming from somewhere inside you that says it's time to forgive and get on with your life.

What if, though, you simply cannot forgive the offender? Maybe you've already tried and failed. More likely you get totally angry at that person every time you think about him or her. You still have a couple options to consider that might help you not let the offender have free rent in your brain. *Distraction* is one possibility. You do that by staying busy, making yourself think of other things, and generally getting on with your life. The other choice is to set a goal of achieving *emotional indifference* toward the offense and offender. This occurs when you can remember what happened without getting all emotional about it.

One reason some people avoid forgiveness work is because they mistakenly believe that they must get back into a relationship with the offender if they forgive. That's simply not true. You can forgive someone without reconciling. For example, perhaps a very good friend stole thousands of dollars from you due to a gambling problem. You can choose to forgive that person without having to resume the friendship. Indeed, you'd be naive and gullible ever to let that person near your pocketbook again. Of course, you might choose to become friends again but only after the offender had done a lot to deal with the gambling problem. Reconciliation is built upon trust as well as forgiveness, so you won't want to reconcile until you have good reason to trust.

....................................................................................

**exercise.** Please consider all four options if you are dealing with a particular resentment: distraction, emotional indifference, forgiveness, and reconciliation. Ask yourself which one makes the most sense right now. Then take action to start moving that way.

....................................................................................

More in **Practices and Examples** at http://20290.nhpubs.com

# 26 The Anger-Turned-Inward and Self-Forgiveness Challenges

## What You Need to Know

It's easy to think of anger problems only when someone directs their anger against others. An example of anger against the self, also called *anger turned inward*, would be the inability to forgive yourself.

Anger against yourself often takes five forms:

1. *Self-neglect*, for example, not bothering to make doctor appointments for yourself because you're too busy taking care of others. The message in self-neglect is that basically you believe that you're not worth caring about.

2. *Self-sabotage*, a way to ensure you don't succeed in life. You're sabotaging yourself when you "pull defeat from the jaws of victory," meaning that you find creative ways to fail just before you would succeed at some task or goal.

3. *Self-blame*, which occurs when you convict yourself of being responsible for anything bad that happens. It's as if you carry around a sign saying, "I'm bad. I'm evil. I'm worthless."

4. *Self-attack*, represented both by saying mean things about yourself to yourself and perhaps by physically harming your body.

5. *Self-destruction*, for example, suicide attempts. Here you believe that you must destroy yourself because of your intrinsic badness.

........................................................................................

**exercise.** How familiar are you with these five forms of anger turned inward? Can you think of recent examples in which you harmed yourself in one or more of these ways by turning your anger inward?

........................................................................................

## Taking It Further

Anger turned inward is most difficult to correct when it reflects a person's inability to forgive himself or herself.

Jerome, formerly a violent man, says he can never forgive himself for having beaten his children. Claudia, a recovering alcoholic, says she could never forgive herself for the years she neglected her children when she was in the midst of her addiction. They have both changed, though. Neither is abusive or neglectful anymore. So why can't they forgive themselves and move on?

Self-forgiveness is difficult because unforgiving people are often haunted by both guilt and shame. Guilt is about transgression, going too far, and violating another's rights. Shame is about failure, not going far enough, and falling short of your values and goals. People who cannot forgive themselves feel guilty because, like Jerome, who beat his kids, they did something bad to others. They feel ashamed because they didn't do something good, like Claudia, who neglected her children. And in reality both Jerome and Claudia probably feel both guilt and shame because the two are so easily intertwined.

When you combine guilt, shame, and disbelief, you end up with a person who cannot self-forgive because "I must keep punishing myself for having been such a horrible person." Notice that somehow the past has infiltrated the present. It's not that "I was a bad person" so much as an underlying belief that "I still am a bad person." To someone who cannot self-forgive, the past is never actually in the past.

........................................................................................

**exercise.** So how can you put the past in the past where it belongs? One way is to create a ritual you can repeat regularly to yourself. This ritual follows a "that was then and this is now" format. Jerome's might look like this:

> "Then I hit the kids. Now I hug them."

> "Then I was proud of my toughness. Now I'm proud of my gentle spirit."

> "Then I was selfish and greedy. Now I try to be generous and thoughtful of others."

Here's Claudia's:

> "Then I neglected my kids. Now I take good care of them."

> "Then I drank myself stupid. Now I'm sober and smarter."

> "Then I fell short of my values. Now I'm living up to my goals and beliefs."

Accept what you did in the past while celebrating the good person you are today.

........................................................................

More in **Practices and Examples** at http://20290.nhpubs.com

# Concluding Remarks

You may want to read more on anger than we've written in this short volume. Here are a few books on this topic that we've written, all published by New Harbinger:

- *Angry All the Time.* 2nd ed. 2005. This is a good book if you know you have a serious anger problem.

- *Letting Go of Anger.* 2nd ed. 2006. Learn about eleven ways people handle their anger.

- *Stop the Anger Now.* 2001. This is a workbook with many practical exercises.

- *Working Anger.* 1998. Learn about anger in the workplace.

We hope you will use the twenty-six chapters in this book to help you manage your anger well. More than that, we believe that when you handle your anger well, you'll have a better life, one with less agitation, anxiety, and negativity and more full of peacefulness, serenity, calmness, and goodwill.

**Ronald T. Potter-Efron, PhD, LCSW,** is a psychotherapist in private practice in Eau Claire, WI, who specializes in anger management. He is author of *Angry All the Time* and coauthor, with Patrick Fanning, of *Letting Go of Anger.*

**Patricia S. Potter-Efron, MS,** is a clinical psychotherapist at First Things First Counseling Center in Eau Claire, WI.

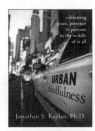